Out of the Darkness and Into the Light

Chapter 1

It was a Wednesday evening in August 2017 and I was on cloud nine. I worked for an amazing team, had a supportive family, and was accepted into a prestigious program I worked two hard years to get into. I was excited to start this new chapter in my life as it was the biggest accomplishment I had to date and it was about to change for the better! However, I had some unsettled fear that I had suppressed deep down about the "unknown". This school had a commute that was over an hour. It would be like a full-time job and would last for two years. I was worried… How would I be able to pay bills? How would I be able to provide for my family? Would my daughter be cared for the way I would care for her?

Speaking of Elaina, she was the light of my world. She was about to turn four years old and was the sweetest little thing I had ever known. She was kind, gentle, funny, and loved to cuddle, which is what we were doing. I was in deep thought as I mindlessly played Backgammon on the tablet. I was sitting on the couch and Elaina was laying her head in my lap watching TV. I was mesmerized by her sweetness and would easily get distracted just looking at her.

I was gently playing with her hair when a sudden panic and a strong sense of guilt came out of nowhere. I'm about to start school in a couple of weeks and instead of playing with my daughter, I was wasting my time on a stupid tablet. The guilt was so strong that I decided to put it away, sit with my daughter, and give her my full attention hoping the panic would disappear. After about an hour, the panic somewhat eased to "bearable", but now it was bedtime. So, I dressed her for bed, laid her down, and knelt beside her to pray. What happens next, I can only hope to explain in the pages to follow.

Chapter 2

Right before I began to pray, I had an overwhelming sense of fear come over me. It felt like something was watching us through my daughter's bedroom window. You know, like out of a horror movie. Like something lurking in the dark, ready to attack and kill for no apparent reason. Now, there have been many times in the past when I felt scared of the dark, or something was under my bed when I was little, or something was hiding in the closet. The kind of fear that comes after watching a scary movie. I stopped watching horror movies years ago, so that wasn't the reason. Besides, this was… different. The feeling I had felt wasn't an eerie fear. It was demonic. Pure evil is the only way I could explain it. However, as I felt this instant evil lurking outside my daughter's window, I quickly remembered I saw the preview for the newest “It” movie. If you don’t know what that is, it is about an evil clown that does horrifically disgusting things. That’s all I have to say, except I strongly encourage you NOT to watch it if you haven’t already. (Please remember this when reading the last chapter and I will explain.)

I don’t know how long it took me to come back to the present moment, but I came back to reality, and I still needed to pray over my daughter. So, I did and I internally “wished” that evil feeling outside the window to go away. But, as I stopped praying, the exact opposite happened. I experienced something for the first time in my life. I kissed my daughter goodnight, trying to ignore whatever was "lurking" outside the window. As I stood up, I FELT (I did not see) the evil thing as it came through the window, passed over my daughter's bed, and entered into my body!

Trying to keep my composure not wanting to alarm my sweet girl, I said "Goodnight". But before I left her room, I remembered a story from a stand-up comedian. It was about him and his family watching a scary movie. When they went to bed, they heard a creepy noise, he ran down the stairs, outside the front door, and hid in his car. The "funny" part of the story was that he realized he had left his wife and kids to defend themselves from the creepy noise.

At that moment, as I was standing in her room I asked myself… "Would I run and leave Elaina to defend herself if we were in a dangerous situation? Could she feel what I was feeling? Did that evil thing enter her body too?!"

I tried telling myself, "No, I would never leave her behind to defend herself. I would kill myself before I ever did that. Wait a minute… What am I saying? I don't want to die! I don't want to kill myself! Why in the world would I even think of such a horrible thing?!"

I started pacing the hallway, trying to figure out what just happened. "Why do I feel this way? Why am I having these thoughts? What in the world was that evil thing that entered my body?! I could still feel it! How do I get it to go away?!" But, within seconds it got worse. Now, I was hearing a voice that wasn't mine!

Chapter 3

"Well, what are you waiting for?" the voice said. As sheer panic ran through my body, I internally replied "Who is this? Waiting for what?" Not answering my questions, the voice became more urgent "Get rid of her. Put a pillow over her head and it will be done". Strangely, I had an urge to listen to the voice. As soon as I felt the urge, I shrieked back in fear and ran away from her room as fast as I could and into my bedroom. "I would never hurt Elaina! I never have and I never will. Why am I thinking this? How do I get this out of my head?" I continued to ask myself internally. "Coward", the voice responded. "Get away from me!", I thought as I paced around my bedroom floor. Then I heard, "You could just kill yourself and then you wouldn't have any more worries". "No more worries…? That sounds nice for a change," I thought while feeling relief. "Wait a minute! NO! I don't want to kill myself. I've never wanted to die and I don't plan to now," I replied.

My husband was asleep in bed. I didn't want to disturb him, but I was terrified of what I was hearing and that the urge to hurt Elaina or myself would come back. I gently shook him hoping he would wake up, but he rolled away. "Don't waste your time. He's not going to help you", the voice said. "Oh yes, he is!" I screamed back. I shook Tyler harder. "Wa…wake up please" came out in a stutter. He rumbled something I couldn't understand. "Wake up," I said urgently. He rolled over and looked at me annoyed. I don't know what my face was saying, but it got his attention. His annoyed expression quickly turned into concern as he asked "What's wrong?" I couldn't find the words to explain what I was hearing or feeling. I couldn't say anything at all and started crying.

"He will never believe you if you tell him", the voice said. Never seeing me like this, Tyler's full attention was on me asking what he could do to help. In fear of what he might think if I told him, I quietly replied, "I'm just having some anxiety. Will you stay awake with me"? He said, "Sure, but I have to pee first." Fear settled in as he went to the bathroom. Trying to distract myself from the intense fear, I searched for something funny to watch on TV. I loved to laugh and it always had been an escape for me. So, over the recent years, I made a point every day to make sure I laughed multiple times a day to prevent any anxiety and it worked. Until now.

The fear slightly eased as he came back to lay on the bed. “As long as he is awake, he won’t let me do any harm”, I thought to myself. He asked me what I wanted to watch once he realized I didn’t want to talk. I have no idea what he turned on as my mind was preoccupied with what was happening to me. Somehow, I found myself mindlessly watching horses peacefully run across a pasture on TV and eventually drifted off to sleep.

Chapter 4

Now I Know What They Were Feeling.

Growing up, life was uneventful. It took a long time for me to realize it, but we were poor. We didn't have a lot, but I didn't know that until middle school. However, we never did without. I have an older brother and a younger sister and we always had clothes on our backs, food on the table, and plenty of kids to play with outside.

I was shy growing up and did not speak unless someone else spoke to me first. Even then, I still spoke quietly unless I was around my family. But, I remember that I was happy on the inside.

I remember being mostly independent and playing by myself a lot if no one else wanted to play with me. I thought everyone around me was just as happy as I was on the inside and that everyone else felt the same things that I did.

I would daydream about traveling and seeing all the exciting things the world had to offer. If it had anything to do with adrenaline, I wanted to experience it! I wanted to go skydiving, scuba diving, riding a hot air balloon, surfing, riding a horse running as fast as it could, and ride all the big rides at Six Flags, etc. I wanted to see the mountains, the vibrant fall trees in the North, and to go on a cruise while watching whales. I wanted to know what it was like to fly on an airplane and visit all 50 states. I wanted to visit every country that I had heard of to experience their culture and try the food they eat. The list never ended. If someone mentioned something new and exciting, I wanted to experience it. Apart from that, I daydreamed of being a momma, taking my kiddos to their extracurricular activities, and experiencing fun things.

In the 5th grade, I decided that I either wanted to be someone who "made pretty teeth" or I wanted to remodel kitchens and bathrooms. If I wasn't daydreaming about experiencing new things, I would have random visions of kitchens and bathrooms pop up in my head. I would spend a lot of time rearranging or changing the vision until I was happy with it. I even started drawing the visions on paper.

Long story short, after all the daydreaming and visions, I got married in 2010, became a dental assistant in May 2012, and a year later, I had my sweet girl, Elaina. It wasn't what I had dreamed of, but I was proud that I went to college, got a degree, and was a momma! This was a big deal for me because most of my family never went to college, let alone finish high school.

But, during all of this and growing up, I never believed in evil things. I refused to believe in evil spirits and only believed in good and happy things. I have seen many horror movies. Not by my choice, but usually my family or friends and I would just play along. I remember having nightmares about Chucky when I was little and I've lost count of how many nightmares I had about the three witches on Hocus Pocus. But, regardless of when I was awake, I refused to believe and found a way to ignore the thoughts. I remember my friends pushing me to the front of the line when going through a haunted house or forest. I remember feeling brave during those moments. I was ready to "protect" my friends by giving my best throat punch if something tried to hurt us. I also did my best not to jump if something popped out to scare us.

I also grew up never understanding why someone would want to hurt or kill themselves. It made me so sad. I would think to myself, "Aren't they as excited as I am about experiencing new things? Why are they cutting their wrist? Why would they jump off a roof without a cable cord or parachute?" But, here I am feeling all of these feelings at once. I now understand exactly what those people felt. I was overwhelmed with sympathy and empathy knowing how hard it is to fight off the voice inside my head. They must have heard this voice, too.

Chapter 5

"Wow, I'm glad that is over. What a nightmare", I said internally. It was the next morning and I was lying in bed grateful to start a new day. "Who said it was over", the voice said. The intense panic came back with an adrenaline rush this time. I jumped out of bed "NO! Go away"! "What are you waiting for? Hurry and get it done while he is sleeping", the voice replied. I looked over at my husband sleeping. I contemplated waking him up again, but I needed to get dressed for work. Doing my best to ignore the voice, I went into the bathroom to get ready. As I entered the bathroom, I could feel and almost see a dark cloud hovering around me. The panic increased. I heard, "You are wasting time".

"What's happening to me?" I knew what an anxiety attack felt like. I had more than I can count growing up. But, it was always in fear that I was sick or going to die. But I've never had a voice talking to me before, let alone telling me to do the very thing I was afraid of all these years. This is different. I feel like I don't have control over my thoughts. It was very overwhelming and I could tell it wouldn't be easy to get rid of this voice. "Is this what it feels like to be possessed? Having a voice telling you what to do. I feel like a puppet. NO! I don't want to be possessed", I shrieked. There's no way I was about to give in. "No, this is stupid. It isn't real and things like this don't happen in real life", I refused. I finished getting ready and went to check on my daughter.

I walked toward her room and heard, “Now is your chance”. I ran away from her room in fear as I yelled “Stop”! I needed to get Elaina ready for daycare. I didn’t have time for this nonsense. I walked back to her room and gently shook her awake. She was so sweet lying there with her hair in a frizz ball and the blankets halfway off the bed. “Hi momma”, she said softly rubbing the sleep out of her eyes. “Good morning, baby. It’s time to wake up”, I said as I stroked her hair. I stood up to get her clothes out of the closet and laid them on the bed.

Suddenly, I could sense two hands coming toward her throat as if they were going to choke her. But, I wasn’t close enough to touch her and my hands were still holding onto her clothes. “What are you waiting for”, the voice said as the hands that weren't mine disappeared. The fear mixed with an increase of adrenaline was causing me to feel nauseous and weak. "Okay, baby. I'll be right back. Take a minute or two and then try to go potty", I said with a weak voice and walked out of her room.

I ran back to my bedroom and paced around the floor trying to understand what I saw. I was hearing a voice that definitely wasn't mine and now I'm seeing strange visions of me hurting Elaina. Except it wasn't me. I don't think. What do I do now? That seemed very real and until I can figure out how to get it to go away, I obviously can't be alone with her.

Tyler was still asleep. I needed him to take Elaina so that I wouldn't have a chance to hurt her. "Don't wake him up. You know he is not a morning person and you will be late", the voice said. I tried to ignore the voice, but whoever he…she, "it" was, was completely right. Who is this voice anyway? I took a minute to ponder if it was a male or female voice I was hearing, but it didn't sound like my squirrely Southern voice. It was a stern, confident voice with an authoritative tone. "Eh, I don't have time for you, whoever you are", I said as I tried waking my husband up.

"Hey, will you please take Elaina to daycare for me?" He didn't budge. "Tyler"! He rolled over and groaned "What's wrong"? "Please take Elaina to Daycare for me," I said with a shaky voice. "What? Why? It's on your way to work" he grumbled as he rolled back over. The fear increased. I knew it sounded silly to ask him when I knew he was right. “Get it together,” I told myself. I don’t remember how I managed to finish getting ready and out of the house on time with Elaina. I just know I did my best to focus on each task in that moment trying to distract myself from fear. I was on autopilot.

“I can do this,” I thought as I pulled out of the driveway and eased down the road. I felt very weak and shaky. “That’s because you are weak. Just run off into the ditch and you won’t have to worry anymore”, the voice said. I thought I was going to be sick. Never once have I had the thought to run off the road. So why is this popping in my head now?

Driving as slowly as I could, I tightened my grip on the steering wheel and focused on staying between the yellow and white lines. I had never been so grateful that her daycare was only five minutes away from the house. In a blur, we made it safely to the daycare with no incident. “Whoo! We made it. What relief!” “This time”, I heard. Another surge of adrenaline shook throughout my body. I got her out and took her in as fast as I could thinking she would be safer with them than with me.

I felt a glimmer of relief once I got back in the car and drove to work. It was a ten-minute drive, that felt much longer. Whenever I crossed an intersection or a bridge, I was terrified that the voice would urge me to do something I didn't want. Thankfully, I made it there safely.

I was thankful for the distraction and the workload as it gave me something to focus on every time my mind would drift back to what I was secretly going through. I also felt safe because I was around people and thought surely they wouldn't let anything dangerous happen. Right? I also noticed that I didn't hear the voice all morning. That's the key! I will just make sure that I'm always around someone and Elaina and I will be safe.

It was lunchtime. I had no appetite, but Stan, my brother worked around the corner so I decided to go see him. There were many times I would go to him for advice or he would come help me when I was in need. Maybe he would understand what was going on with me.

It was a quick two-minute drive. "He's not going to believe you", I heard. NO! I've done well all morning. I needed to hurry and get inside so the voice would go away. The look on Stan's face was something between concern and surprise. I must have pushed through the office door harder than I meant to. "Hey, sister. What are you up to?" I sat down in front of him, trying to catch the breath that I was apparently holding and secretly trying to calm my racing heartbeat.

I wanted to blurt out everything that had happened, but I couldn't speak. "Are you ok?" He asked. I shook my head "Yes, I'll be right back". I went to the rest room trying to contemplate how I was going to explain all of this. Honestly, I didn't even want to think about it anymore. I wanted it to go away and for me to carry about my happy self and the exciting journey that I'm about to start.

"You're not going to tell him. He won't understand. He will try to make you feel better, but it won't work." This was tough. Are these my thoughts or is the voice trying to scare me? Either way, it's true. Even if I did my best to explain it to him, he would never understand. It was too much for me, so I could only imagine what he would think. I came out of the restroom but sat in an empty room with the lights off. I cried quietly, wishing all of this away. I needed to focus on work before I go to orientation next week.

"You okay sister?" Stan said as he quietly approached me. I couldn't speak. He turned on the lights. I looked away and demanded that my tears go away. All of a sudden I felt embarrassed that I was crying in front of my brother. It wasn't something that I did often. Maybe not ever except maybe at a funeral. "Talk to me. What's wrong."

"I'm not sure", I whispered. I'm surprised I could speak at all. Those who know me well, know I can't talk if I'm about to cry. It will cause the floodgates to open and strange wailing noises come out rather than words.

"Come on. You know you will feel better if you talk." He isn't wrong. Nine times out of ten, I felt better if I talked to get something off my chest. "Not this time", I heard the voice say. Trying to stay calm I said, "Um, well… do you think people can be possessed"? He looked at me a moment, "Yes. Why do you ask". The fear and adrenaline rush spiked as I screamed internally, "NO! I don't want to be possessed".

"Well, I've always thought things like that were a myth or in horror films just to scare people," I said gauging to see if he would think I was crazy. "But, I think that maybe…" I could barely talk. I didn't want it to be true. "Maybe what?" He said. "Do you think I am possessed?" I asked. He paused for a second, "Oh no. You couldn't be", he said. "Oh thank goodness", I thought internally as I felt instant relief at his confidence. "But, how do you know for sure?" I asked him. "Because you would be out doing crazy things if you were," he said as he walked off. He had a customer come in he needed to tend to.

Dang, well now I'm not sure. He said I would be out doing crazy things. Even though I haven't done anything, he doesn't know the things I'm hearing or seeing are tempting me to do these crazy things. Ugh, this was too much and it's almost time to go back to work. I waited until his customer left and I went to his desk to sit in front of him. We talked for a few more minutes before I had to leave.

The rest of the day went quickly. Though I was still scared about what was happening, what my brother said gave me a glimmer of hope that I was not possessed. I haven't done anything thank goodness. But, it still doesn't explain why I am thinking these things. Surely, if it's my thoughts and I don't act on them, they will just go away. Right?

Chapter 6

I was wrong. The thoughts didn't go away. They got worse. I was convinced it was not my thoughts. The only reason I knew for sure is because I knew myself and the way I think. The things I would think were contradictory to the things I heard and was scared of.

For the next three days, I was terrified to be alone with Elaina. I would continue to hear the voice I wanted to get rid of so badly, tempting me to do things I had never seen in a horror movie. It was Friday and I didn't have to work. However, for the first time ever, I didn't want to spend the day with Elaina. I didn't want to spend all day listening to a voice tempting me to hurt my daughter and no one else was around. So, I gathered as much bravery as I could and took her to daycare only five minutes away.

I also didn't want to stay by myself all day in fear of the voice tempting me to kill myself. Surely, if I am with someone I wouldn't act on it. So, I decided to go to work with Tyler that day. I had no idea what he was going to be doing and I didn't care. I needed to be around someone and I needed a distraction.

We were at his parent's house cleaning out their garage. It needed a typical cleaning and to be reorganized from things being piled up like it was a game of Jenga. I was in a daze and on autopilot. I haven't had any rest in the last two days and lost my appetite, which wasn't like me because I love food.

I still haven't told Tyler anything. I wasn't sure that he would understand. "That's because he won't" the voice interrupted my daze. Fear raced through my body at the words only I could hear. I tried to keep my outward appearance calm and I started to clean faster to distract myself.

I came across a yellow DeWalt drill. I started to pick it up until I heard, "Yes. Get the drill and drill it into the back of Tyler's neck. He will never see it coming". "Wait, what?" I said internally. I looked up at Tyler's neck. He was facing away from me. I had a quick vision of my hand grabbing the drill and pushing it into the back of his neck. Except it wasn't my hands. My hands were clenched tight by my side and were turning white. It felt like my heart was going to jump out of my chest as a new and stronger surge of anxiety ran through my arms and legs. I'm going to be sick!

I wasn't able to hide my reaction this time. I ran away from the drill as fast as I could where he couldn't see me, crying and hyperventilating. I knew I needed to calm down as fast as I could. I didn't want Tyler to see me like this and start asking questions I couldn't answer. There was no way I was about to tell him what I just saw and felt tempted to do. I couldn't tell anyone that. Or, the things I heard when I was alone with Elaina.

I took a few deep breaths to calm my nerves and blotted my eyes dry the best I could. I don't know how long I was gone, but Tyler eventually found me. He looked concerned as he asked, “What’s wrong”? “I’m okay. I’m just having a rough morning.” “Are you sure you don’t want to go home and relax?” He asked me still looking concerned. My anxiety increased at the thought of being by myself. “No, really I want to be here. I just needed a little break. Let’s keep going”, I said wanting to break away from this conversation before it went any further.

We continued cleaning for a couple more hours before heading home. I avoided any drills and cleaned up as far away from Tyler as possible until I came across a hammer. “This should work. Just bash it in the back of his head”, I heard. I started to see the vision of me picking up the hammer. “NO!”, I screeched to myself. “Go away!”, I screamed at the vision as I turned to pick up trash and threw it in a bag. I started cleaning faster again, focusing on each object I picked up steering clear of all tools this time.

I was back in a daze as I cleaned and stayed quiet. Strangely I was grateful for the daze. It was better than hearing voices in my head. Thankfully, I didn't hear the voice the rest of our time cleaning and rearranging. But, I had an overwhelming anxiety that I couldn't get rid of. My whole body was tense and in defense mode as I walked around trying to act normal.

We went home, but we still had a couple of hours before Elaina needed to be picked up. I knew I needed to eat something before my blood sugar dropped and feel queasy. I didn't have an appetite, so I just found a small snack to tide me over.

I concluded that if I had at least two adults around me, everyone would be safe regardless of what the voice said. Since it was Friday, I asked my mom if she wanted to come over to hang out after work. I immediately felt relief when she said yes.

The rest of the evening went by smoothly even though I was still struggling inside. I had an invisible dark cloud hovering over me and I still felt a constant sense of anxiety that I couldn't shake. But, I was thankful for the company and what little distraction it gave me. Which was gone as soon as Mom said she was leaving. I tried my best not to let her see my fear as she walked out the door.

I didn't want her to feel obligated to stay. I was a grown adult and should be able to get a grip on the situation. Right?

I hurried as fast as I could to put Elaina in bed before any thoughts or voices interrupted me. I got in bed as fast as possible and turned on a Jeff Foxworthy special hoping the humor would distract me while I fell asleep. Thankfully, it did as I dozed off 20 minutes later from exhaustion.

Chapter 7

I woke up the next morning. I was desperately hoping that it was all a nightmare and it was over. Until I heard, "What are you waiting for"? No, not again! I rolled over and closed my eyes. Maybe I could fall back asleep to avoid the voice and the anxiety that just spiked to a nine.

But as soon as I closed my eyes, I began to see dark, distorted figures coming toward me. One figure had a dark gray face with spikey-looking thorns coming out of its face, red glowing eyes, sharp teeth that resembled nails, long pointed ears that bent backward, and sharp claws that were surging towards me like it was going to strangle me.

My anxiety shot to a 20 as I quickly sat up. "What was that"? I said internally. "What are you waiting for?" I heard. I laid back down and pulled the covers over my head and closed my eyes. This time I saw multiple creepy black figures as if they were shadows. Some had red glowing eyes and others I couldn't tell what they looked like. My anxiety turned to panic as they all came rushing toward me with arms and claws stretched out toward me.

I jumped up out of bed in defense mode to protect myself from the figures. But there wasn't anyone in the room, except Tyler, asleep in the bed.

It was still early. I walked quietly and quickly to check on Elaina. She was safe and asleep in her bed. My panic eased up so I took a shower and brushed my teeth.

As I started to brush my teeth, my fear increased as I looked in the mirror. I could see a faint, dark cloud or fog surrounding me. I quickly looked away as my anxiety increased. Maybe it was just my imagination. Regardless, I was scared to look back in the mirror, afraid that I might begin to see something worse. I was afraid I might see something in myself that didn't look like my true reflection. I could also feel something lurking in the bathroom, but I didn't intend to find out. I just wanted it to go away. I finished brushing my teeth and went to the kitchen.

There were dirty dishes in the sink. Saturday mornings were my reset days and I was a morning person. Everyone was still asleep so I decided to take advantage and do a quick clean. I quickly threw away any trash, wiped off the counters, put the remaining dishes in the sink, and swept the floor.

As I started the dishes, I immediately began to panic when I heard, “This knife will work”. I was holding a butcher knife and a vision of me cutting my left wrist, then jabbing it into my stomach flashed before me. I instantly dropped the knife and ran out of the kitchen.

I paced back and forth through the hallway. My heart was racing, my chest began to feel tight, and I couldn’t tell if I was going to pass out or throw up. “What’s happening to me?!” I screamed internally as I put my hands on my head. “I don’t want to die”, I began to cry.

How was I supposed to get anything done if I kept having a panic attack every time I got close to someone or a potential weapon? "Get it together," I told myself. I tried to ignore the fear and press on. I went to finish the dishes, but the fear increased when I saw the knife. So, I decided to hide the dirty knives and wait for Tyler to wash them later. It helped relieve some of the tension I didn't realize I had once they were hidden and I was able to finish the rest.

What do I do now? I didn't want to be alone with Elaina and knew she would wake up soon. I wanted to call my family to ask if they wanted to come back over, but the only one that would be awake at this hour was my dad and he was working. So, I decided to wait a while longer.

"Mommy", I heard Elaina's sweet voice coming from her room. But, I started to panic about being alone with her and was afraid I would hear the voice again.

I got her up, let her potty, and made her breakfast as quickly as I could while trying to distract myself from the fear that was slowly increasing. I let her eat on the couch and watch cartoons while staying as far away from her as I could doing random chores to stay occupied.

Thankfully, my family decided to come hang out later. I knew they would start asking questions if I kept inviting them over every day. I needed to figure something else out.

It was like this for the next several days. For three days, I was completely terrified to be alone with Elaina; I kept hearing the voice telling me to use random objects to hurt myself or someone else; I was too afraid to look in the mirror; I could feel something lurking near me everywhere I went, and my anxiety would spike or I would have a panic attack every 5-10 minutes when these things would happen. Also, when I closed my eyes I would see the dark, creepy figures launching towards me. I had to watch something funny to fall asleep to every night so I didn't have to lay there with my eyes closed. When would this go away?

Chapter 8

Somehow, I got through all of the panic and anxiety for those several days. However, it was my first day of orientation at Texas Woman's University (TWU) and I had an hour commute. I wanted to be excited. I worked so hard to get to this point and after two long, hard years of working non-stop to get into a dental hygiene program, the first day was finally here. But, with everything going on my joy was gone and it was replaced with a constant state of anxiety.

I got to school safely. I knew my dad would be awake so I called and talked to him most of the drive. I made it through orientation solely on autopilot. Most of my classmates seemed happy and excited to get started. "I wish I felt as happy as they look", I thought. We had some group activities to help break the ice, get to know each other, and for team building. I felt guilty for not giving it my all. Normally, I loved doing activities, having fun, and working as a team. Unfortunately, I didn't have anything emotionally or mentally left to give. It had been sucked out of me. I almost felt lifeless and it took all the energy I had to focus on what the professors were saying.

The first day was over and it was time to go home. I walked in a daze to my car. At this point, I was void of any energy. My mind was overstimulated from orientation even though we were sitting all day and not exerting any physical energy. I felt weak.

I had a long drive home, was tired, and wanted to lie down. Until a surge of anxiety and adrenaline shot through me when I heard, “What are you waiting for, just do it”. I haven’t heard the voice all day until now.

I was two miles away from the school and realized I needed a distraction to help me get home. This time, I called my mom. She was at work, but thankfully she answered.

“Hey, baby. How was orientation?” she asked. I don’t know how she did it, but she knew my and my sibling's schedule, even though we are all adults. “Courtney?” I realized I hadn’t responded. “Hey”, I uttered. I couldn’t hardly talk. “Crap she is going to know something is wrong. She ALWAYS knows”, I thought to myself.

"Honey, what's wrong?" she said. "I'm just tired and I probably need to eat something", I said. Another surge of anxiety, panic, and adrenaline ran through me as I realized I hadn't eaten in 24 hours. That was impossible. Normally, I would get sick and lightheaded if I didn't eat breakfast. I started to cry. The adrenaline and anxiety were too much to handle at this point.

"Courtney, I need you to talk to me", mom said urgently. She knows I can't talk if I'm crying, so she gave me a minute and ordered me to start talking. Once I could speak, I uttered, "Mom, I don't know what is wrong with me. You know I easily get sick if I don't eat and I just realized I haven't eaten in 24 hours". I was sobbing now and I could barely see from all the tears pooling in my eyes. Maybe it isn't a big deal to other people, but nutrition and fueling my body were important to me.

I was in a daze again when I heard multiple cars honking. I wiped my eyes and took a deep breath trying to calm myself. The honking got louder. I looked around to see what was happening and realized I was rolling into oncoming traffic at a stop light. I was so focused on the crippling anxiety and trying to calm myself that I didn't notice that I had let my foot off the brake. I was rolling about 5mph, but I was already halfway through the stoplight, so I decided to speed up and finish getting through the light. I started to cry harder and pulled over.

I couldn't take it anymore. This was too much. I could have hurt or worse KILLED someone! Mom was saying something, but I was hyperventilating and couldn't understand her. "Why are you fighting so hard? Just get it over with and you won't have to deal with it anymore", the voice interrupted my crying. Another surge of panic, if you could imagine, ran through me while I was hyperventilating.

"Mmm Mom", I stuttered. "I can't do this anymore. I'm so tired." "What's going on?!" raising her voice. I explained that I ran through a red light and the guilt I was having. She spent a few minutes trying to calm me down. Once I felt safe and calm enough to drive, I headed home. My guilt somewhat turned into gratitude that I didn't hurt anyone. I definitely couldn't have handled that.

Mom stayed on the phone with me for the hour-long drive home. I got home safely, but I was completely drained. I don’t remember most of the evening, but I forced myself to eat something small and then had to lie down.

The next several days were filled with visions of dark creepy things when I closed my eyes, trying to avoid any and every sharp potential weapon, and doing my best to stay on the phone or in the same room with one or more adults with me. My family knew something was wrong, but there was no way I could tell them what was going on in my mind. Right?

Chapter 9

"The gun in the hallway, you could use that and get it done much quicker", the voice said. I was driving home from school the next day. It had only been two weeks since this all started. You would think I would be used to hearing a random voice prompting me to do awful things, but I wasn't. I would have a new surge of anxiety and panic attacks cut through an ongoing dull anxiety that lingered throughout the day. This time was no different.

I knew exactly what the voice was implying because I had a vivid vision flash before me showing me what to do. There was a rifle, zipped up in a canvas sleeve and the sleeve was in an old gun cabinet with a glass door located in the hallway. In the vision, I was going to take it out, shoot Tyler, and then shoot myself. “But, why”, I thought to myself and I took deep breaths to calm my anxiety. “So you won’t have to work so hard anymore. You’re weak and tired”, the voice replied.

I shrank back from the voice trying to find a way to distract myself. I didn’t understand. Why am I suddenly hearing things that I have never, not once, had the desire to do? Let alone being prompted to do followed by a vision of how to do it. But, the voice was right. I do feel weak and I was very tired. For a brief moment, the thought sounded appealing. “WAIT! NO!” I screamed and started to cry when I realized dying sounded appealing. I don’t want to die! A stronger wave of panic shot through me as I tried to analyze and reason with myself. I failed to calm myself down. So, I called my mom to talk to her for the rest of the drive home, hoping it would help calm and distract me.

I made it home safely but didn't want to get out of the car. I was afraid to go in or anywhere near the gun cabinet. It was in the hallway, between the master bedroom and Elaina's room, and no way to avoid it. I took a few minutes to gather up the courage and slowly walked through the back door trying to avoid eye contact with the cabinet. I went to the bedroom and put my stuff down.

I needed to go check in on Elaina, but now I was afraid to leave the bedroom, afraid the voice would prompt me to open the gun case. "This is stupid. I'm not going to do that. I would never hurt someone. Get it together, Courtney", I scolded myself. I straightened up, prepped myself, and opened the bedroom door. I took a deep breath, ran, and leaped as far as I could past the gun cabinet like I was in the Russian Ballet. "Real smooth, Courtney. Real smooth." I didn't care, I felt relief once I got past the cabinet. Almost… proud of myself.

Unfortunately, the images of taking out the gun and the voice were still telling me reasons why I should use it. The next day I couldn't get the image out of my head and I didn't have the energy to keep leaping through the hallway. I had the perfect solution. On the way home, I called Tyler. "Hello?" "Hey, I need you to take the gun out of that cabinet and hide it somewhere. Don't ever tell me where it is", I said. "What gun?" he replied. "The rifle zipped up in that green canvas thing. You know the one sitting in the large gun cabinet in the hallway? You can't miss it." It was quiet on the other end of the line. "Hello?" "Courtney, I don't know what you're talking about. There isn't a gun in that cabinet." "Yes, there is! It's in that green case" I said, getting impatient. I just wanted the gun out of my sight. "Yes, the green canvas is in there, but there isn't a gun in it. It's empty", he said. "Are you sure?", I said with disbelief. "Yes, I am sure. There hasn't ever been a gun in there. Courtney, what's going on?" "Oh…wow ok. Nothing, I just didn't want one in the house", I said casually like everything was suddenly fine. "Everything is fine. Really. I'll be home soon", I said and hung up.

What a relief! I felt a huge weight lifted off of me and my poor calves. I was panicking, anxious, and worrying about something that didn't exist this whole time?! "Take that!" I said to the voice feeling a small boost of confidence for the first time.

I got home feeling like I had won a small victory with a slight pep in my step. Tyler showed me there was no gun in the green canvas case, which boosted my confidence a little more. I still felt a dark cloud hovering over me, but I was able to relax a little that evening and spend much-needed quality time with Elaina.

Unfortunately, that didn't last long. The voice was relentless in interrupting my thoughts to insert some psychotic task throughout the next few days. There was no gun, but now every sharp object was suddenly highlighted as a weapon, and how to use it to hurt Tyler, Elaina, or myself.

I desperately wanted to feel normal and forced myself to do normal tasks hoping to find some relief. I decided I would try to cook dinner one evening, trying to stay away from Tyler and Elaina. However, the voice found ways to interrupt that task by prompting me to burn myself on the hot stove. I stepped back in fear for a few moments, gathered my feelings, and pressed on. But, when I opened the oven and felt the heat rush all over me, there was a strong urge to obey the voice by touching the hot surface. I ran out of the kitchen as fast as I could with a crippling panic that took my breath away.

“That’s it”, I thought to myself. I had enough and realized I was going to need help to get through this. I put away my pride and tried to think of the best way to get help. Surely, a doctor would know how to help, right? I made a mental task to go to an urgent care facility the next day right after school.

By this time, I was carpooling with two of my good friends, Livvy and Carly. I welcomed the company as the conversations helped distract me from the constant anxiety. The thought that I was finally going to get help, also eased the fear throughout the day. I lived the furthest away. The routine was to drop off Carly first and then go to Livvy’s house where my car was parked. I love my friends, but on this particular day, I didn’t stick around long enough to chat. I desperately needed to find help to get rid of… well, whatever this voice, fear, anxiety, and panic was.

When I was finally alone and back to my hometown, I immediately drove to the urgent care facility hoping that fear and pride wouldn't have time to change my mind. Thankfully, the facility was only a few minutes away from Livvy's house. Of course, the voice tried to distract me by saying, "They are going to think you are crazy". But, I didn't care. I finally made it here and wasn't backing down now.

The ladies up front welcomed me and asked what brought me there. "They will never believe you", the voice interjected. "I'm having some anxiety", I replied to the receptionist while doubt crept in. She smiled and handed me the paperwork. It didn't take long to get back to the room and for the doctor to come in. It was the end of the day and he looked tired. "The ladies said that you're having some anxiety. Tell me a little more", he said.

I took a few breaths and tried to figure out how I was going to explain this without sounding like the psycho that I started to believe I was. I knew I needed to give him as much truth as I could if I was going to get the proper treatment I needed. I gave the doctor a brief overview but realized I was just babbling when I saw him sit down in a chair as far away from me as possible.

"So… you know that creepy feeling after watching a horror movie? Well, it feels like that, but all of the time. I can't figure out how to make it go away." I gave him a few examples but stopped talking when I saw the doctor smirking behind his hand. It was obvious he was trying not to laugh. "I told you they wouldn't believe you", the voice chimed in. I ignored the voice and hoped there was still a way to make it stop. The doctor prescribed two different medications. One for anxiety and one for depression.

Even though I did not like taking medication, I left the doctor's office feeling hopeful for the first time and started taking it as instructed that evening.

Chapter 10

Something was off. I had taken the two medications that the doctor prescribed about an hour ago. But, somehow I feel worse. I had never taken these medications before and contemplated if it was normal. I decided to find something comforting to do to see if it would get better. Unfortunately, after another hour, other symptoms occurred. I started to feel shaky, my brain became foggy, and my anxiety became unmanageable.

I called my mom to see what she thought I should do and to help me sort through my thoughts. The doctor's office was already closed so she recommended that I call the pharmacy to see if they could give me any information.

It was late, but fortunately, the pharmacy didn't close until 8 pm. So, I called and explained my symptoms to the pharmacist and stressed that it had only been a couple of hours, but I felt much worse. "No, that's not how the medication works. You have to give the medication at least two weeks before you will notice an improvement", the pharmacist replied. Feeling defeated, I thanked him and hung up. Since he was a professional, I decided to take his advice and take the medication as instructed.

The next day, my brain felt so foggy and my thoughts were delayed. My anxiety was still high, but instead of being in "fight or flight" mode, the anxiety came in sluggish waves throughout the day. When I got home, I could feel the waves occur more frequently. I tried my best to distract myself and take my next dose of medication. “I don’t know why you’re trying so hard. This medication can’t help you”, the voice interrupted my evening. All of the sluggish movements and brain fog quickly turned back to fight mode. There was a huge wave of adrenaline that was impossible to tame or control.

Thankfully, the doctor's office was still open. I called and gave them as much information as I could hoping that the doctor could steer me in the right direction or maybe even a different medication. The receptionist put me on a brief hold to talk to the doctor. “I spoke with the doctor and he said that you need to give the medication at least two weeks before you see an improvement”, she said. “But, is it supposed to make me feel worse before it gets better?" I asked. "All he told me was you have to give it two weeks. If it doesn't get better by then, give us a call", she replied. Feeling another round of defeat, I thanked her and hung up.

Trying to find something positive to focus on, I closed my eyes and laid my head in my hands while I sat quietly at the kitchen table. Immediately, dark creepy figures flashed before me with their sharp claws stretched out as if they were going to strangle me. I opened my eyes and jumped up from the table looking around to see if there were figures near me. I didn't see any, but I could sense something hovering around me. Almost like someone standing next to me, yet I saw nothing.

I decided to spend a little time with Elaina playing with building blocks on the floor hoping it would distract me. I went to bed early that evening. I decided to watch stand-up comedy to fall asleep to avoid closing my eyes and seeing the dark figures dash toward me.

The next day during school I felt even more sluggish. So much more that it got my professor's attention. "Are you feeling ok?" She asked. "Oh, yes ma'am", I barely replied. I couldn't hardly find the proper words to speak and I realized the effort it took to say anything. "Are you sure? I don't want to pry, but you seem tired or something", she replied with a concerned look on her face. "Well, I have been dealing with some anxiety and my doctor put me on some medication. I've never taken it before, but I have noticed that my brain feels foggy", I told her with a crooked smile. "Oh, I see. Well, I know that the program can be overwhelming and I know that some medications can make us feel strange. Make sure you listen to what your body is telling you. Have you asked your doctor to see if you can try a different medication?" She asked with a hopeful tone in her voice.

I explained the last two days and that I've talked with the pharmacist and the doctor who prescribed the medications. By this time, the class was dismissed, but she stayed behind to talk with me and speak words of encouragement to me before we left. While I was grateful that she seemed to have a history of medication making her feel strange, I still had some doubts about what to do.

If only she knew what was going on. "Don't tell her. They will think you're crazy and then dismiss you from the hygiene program", the voice said.

What little encouragement I was feeling turned into fear. But, I was convinced in this situation, the voice was right. If they knew what was going on, there was a high possibility that they would deem me unfit to be providing care to patients. "Maybe I shouldn't be providing care while my brain is so foggy", I thought to myself. Even though we were not providing care at that time, I was worried the brain fog wouldn't go away before seeing my first patient.

I was drained by the time I got home that evening. I asked my mom to come over. She sat in the recliner in the living room and I sat on the floor with my arms around my knees. I was hoping her conversation would help distract me from the voice, the strange presence lurking around me, the brain fog.

Suddenly, out of nowhere, I saw a vision of me taking a knife and stabbing my mom repeatedly until she bled to death. Except it didn't look like my hands were stabbing and there was not a knife anywhere near us. I scurried backward across the floor as far away from my mom as I could until my back was against the couch.

I started crying hysterically. With wide eyes, my mom stood to sit next to me. "NO! Stay over there. Stay away from me!" I screamed. She stood there for a moment concerned. "What's wrong?" She asked. "No, you can't come near me" I cried. She sat back down and I could see tears slowly falling down her cheeks. She wanted to help me, but she didn't know how. "Courtney, I need you to talk to me." My sobs became labored and I could hardly catch my breath.

Realizing that it might take me a few minutes to calm down, Mom sat quietly across the room and cried with me. Once I finally calmed down, she urged me to tell her what it wrong. "I can't tell you," I said wiping tears from my face. "Oh, yes you can", she replied.

I took a few more moments and realized she wasn't going to back down until I told her. With my voice trembling, I told her about the vision I had just seen. I looked away from her in shame and started to cry again. I didn't want her to hate me and I didn't want her to be scared of me. But, how was I supposed to spend time with her if I was having these thoughts and visions? "Look at me", she said sternly. "That doesn't scare me."

I started to cry again and looked away. "Look at me", she said again. I looked at her. She had tears in her eyes, but she didn't look afraid. They were tears of sorrow and concern. "I'm not afraid that you will hurt me. That isn't who you are and you would have done it already if it was going to happen", she said.

Somehow, that gave me relief. We both sat in silence for a few moments and then she said, "Now come here and give me a hug". I looked at her in fear. I still didn't feel confident being close to her. "Get up and come here", she urged me. I slowly crawled over to her, got on my knees, and hugged her. She pulled me in tighter and held me for a few minutes while I cried. "See? I told you that you wouldn't hurt me", she said with a smile on her face. I wasn't fully convinced yet, but I did feel a little better. "And don't you ever run away from me in fear again. You can always come to me and talk to me."

It was getting late and I knew she needed to leave. "Do you want me to stay with you tonight?" She asked. "No. I will be ok", I replied. She lingered around a little longer to see if I would change my mind. Finally, I assured her that I would be fine and that I was about to go to sleep. She hugged me again and I walked her to the door.

I took another round of the medication as instructed. I felt so weak that I felt like I needed to lie down. As I lay there on the bed, I felt like I was going to vomit. I tried my best to eat something, but the nausea got worse. I rolled over on my stomach and took deep breaths, wishing the nausea would go away and I finally drifted off to sleep.

Chapter 11

I had a lecture class the next morning. I slowly made my way to the classroom and took my seat. I sat there quietly and drifted off into a daze waiting for our radiology professor to come in. “You look terrible”, my friend said bluntly. She also said it loud enough to snap me out of my daze and draw my classmates’ attention. Oh, Amber. She was the friend you could count on to be blunt and honest, not sparing anyone’s feelings. She was funny and I liked that she wasn’t afraid to speak the truth to your face. Honestly, I admired her for it.

“I look that bad, huh?” I asked, giving her a small grin. “I’m sorry, but seriously…you look pale, you have dark circles under your eyes, and you look skinny”, she replied. I chuckled and I could feel the blood rush to my pale cheeks knowing that all eyes were on me. “Well, I am kind of tired. I’ve had a rough few days”, I said looking away from her. “Well, you need to get that fixed. Get some sleep or something”. I smiled at her. “Yes, ma’am. I agree.”

Unfortunately, by the time I got home, the anxiety escalated so high and I had no energy to combat it. “Just get it over with when you get home and you won’t have to fight anymore”, the voice said. I was almost home when I felt the urge to give in to the voice. I was so tired and I just wanted a break. Even if it meant finding a way to kill myself. “No!!” I screamed. “What am I thinking?!”

I called my mom to see if she would come over. I didn't know what to do. But, I knew I needed her company now more than ever.

I also had no appetite. It was completely gone to the point where I had to force myself to eat which wasn't easy with the nausea I was experiencing from the medication. She said that she would come over as soon as she could.

I didn't want to be alone. When I pulled up to the house, I saw my brother, Stan, had just gotten there. I pulled up as fast as I could and got out. I rushed over to him and hugged him as hard as I could. He awkwardly hugged me back and said, "Hey, hey, it's going to be okay". I felt awkward, too. We weren't the hugging type and I couldn't tell you the last time I had ever hugged him, except maybe at a funeral. But, I didn't care. I hugged him tighter.

"No, you don't understand. I don't want to die!" I cried. He pried my arms off of him and pushed me away at arm's length. "What are you talking about? You're not going to die. You're going to be okay", he said, trying to stay calm for my benefit. "No, no", I shook my head and continued crying. "I can't get it to go away and I'm tired", I cried as I fell forward and put my head on his chest.

Knowing my brother, this made him uncomfortable. But, this time he didn't push me away. He just let me stand there awkwardly, patting my back, not knowing what to say. Finally, I stopped crying for a few seconds when I heard a car coming up the driveway. It was my mom. I pushed away from Stan and ran to get in the car with her.

"What's going on?" she asked, looking back and forth between me and Stan. He shrugged his shoulders at her and they both stared at me. "You want me to take you for a drive?" she asked. "Yes, but Tyler doesn't know that I am home and I need to check on Elaina", I said sobbing. "I can go talk to Tyler and I will check on Elaina for you. You go with mom", Stan said.

Mom sat there for a minute waiting to see what I wanted to do. "I think I have an idea", she said. She took out her phone and called her cousin. "Hey, is Colby there? Oh, okay. Can you give me his number? I want to see if he can pray over Courtney", she said. I looked at her with wide eyes. She ignored me. "Do you think he would? She's…having a hard time" she said, looking back at me. I couldn't hear what was being said on the other end. But after a few words, Mom ended the call and started to dial another number. "Hey, Colby. This is Regina. Courtney is having a hard time and I think she could use some prayers", Mom said. "If you tell them, they will call CPS and take Elaina away from you", the voice said. I started to panic as Mom handed me the phone. I shook my head no and started to cry again. Unfortunately, the voice had a point. If people knew the things that were going on in my head, there was a very BIG possibility they would think I was crazy and not fit to be a mother. The thought was devastating and I started to cry harder.

Mom didn't push me to talk on the phone. I don't remember what she said to Colby, but she hung up and started to back out of the driveway while I continued to sob uncontrollably. She drove slowly down some back roads while I cried. When it seemed like I might be able to catch my breath, the voice would interrupt and speak something about death and then I would begin to cry more. It was a toxic cycle that continued for hours.

At one point I remembered that I had an online exam due that evening. At this point, I only had an hour left to complete it. I've never missed an exam before, but I knew there was no way I was going to be able to focus enough to get it done. I didn't think the anxiety could get any worse at this point, but to my surprise, it escalated a few notches. My heart was pounding and I couldn't decide if I was going to faint or vomit. My vision became blurry, my chest felt heavy, and it felt like invisible walls were closing in on me making me claustrophobic.

I don't know what my body language looked like, but Mom could tell something had gotten worse quickly. Somehow I was able to make a complete sentence through my sobbing and stuttering to explain I had a radiology exam I needed to take. "Can you take it another day? I'm sure your professor will understand", she said calmly. I shrugged my shoulders as I continued to cry. Mom knew I didn't like to put things off, especially when it came to school. I worked too hard to get to this point and I didn't want my professors to think I was lazy or making excuses. “Do you have your professor's phone number?” Mom asked. I pulled my phone out and scanned it until I found the phone number. “Mom I don’t think I can quit crying long enough for her to understand what I am saying”, I stuttered. “It’s okay. I will call and talk to her”, she replied.

Mom called the number I had pulled up on my phone. I heard a small voice answer on the other end. Suddenly, I felt guilty for having my mom call. I hated interrupting people during their family time and it was getting late. “Hello, this is Regina. Courtney’s mother…”, Mom’s voice got quiet. I looked over at her and she had tears rolling down her cheeks. I started to feel even worse. I hated that I was making my mom cry. I couldn’t hear what was being said on the other end. “Courtney is having a hard time and I will be taking her to the ER. But, she’s worried about her exam that is due this evening”, Mom said through her sobbing. “Are you sure? Ok, thank you. I will tell her. Yes, ma’am you have a good evening”, mom said and ended the call. “She told me to make sure you’re taken care of and not to worry about the exam. She will let you take it another day”, Mom said with a half grin.

Thankfully, the pressure in my chest started to ease, I started to catch my breath and calm down a little. “You think I should go to the ER?” I asked. “Well, I’m going to head in that direction and you can make the decision once we get there”, she said. She took her time getting there and took the long way. I continued to cry on the way there. What would I say once I got in there? Would they even believe me? “No. If you tell them, they will think you are crazy. They will call CPS and take Elaina away”, the voice said. My chest tightened as I heard those words, but I agreed. I didn’t want her taken away from me. The thought made me cry harder and I drifted off into deep thought about what my future would look like. More importantly, what would my sweet Elaina’s future look like?

Chapter 12

I came back to the present when I realized Mom was pulling into the ER parking lot. She found a parking spot, turned off the car, and waited for my instructions. My brain was foggy and it was hard to sort through my thoughts. I didn't want to go in, but I felt lost and didn't know what else to do. I continued to cry.

Mom's phone rang. I looked at her and realized she had also been crying with me. She cleared her throat and answered. It was Tyler and his mom calling to check on me. I didn't want to talk, so Mom put them on speakerphone. Mom explained where we were and what we were doing. "Courtney, don't go in there", my mother-in-law said. That statement caught my attention.

"If you go in there, they will take you to the psych ward and they will not let you leave", she continued. I began to cry harder.

No one knew what the voice had been warning me about. I tried to ignore it. But now my mother-in-law was confirming that if I said anything, they were going to think I was crazy. I felt defeated. Hopeless.

I don't remember the rest of the phone conversation, because fear took over and I felt suffocated. Mom finished the conversation and hung up. We sat there for another hour while I cried and contemplated what I should do. Maybe I am psycho since I am hearing voices? Maybe turning myself in is the best option? At least everyone would be protected from me.

At some point, I started to calm down. My mom tried distracting me with small talk, which seemed to help. I looked at the clock and saw that it was already after 9 pm. I apologized for keeping her out so late. She tried reassuring me that she had nothing else to do. But, I knew better and I knew that she hadn't had a chance to eat dinner.

"I think I'm okay now. We can go back home", I said. "Are you sure?", she asked. "Honestly, no. I'm not sure. But it's getting late, I'm tired, and I know you have to be getting tired", I said. She waited a few more minutes while making small talk to see if I would change my mind. "I think I'm okay now. But, I'm not taking any more of those medications. I don't care what the doctor and pharmacist said. I can tell it is making everything worse. I think I will give it a few days and then see if I feel any better", I said trying to convince her I was okay. "Okay. Well, let's get you home then", she replied.

The next few days were a blur. The voice and the intrusive thoughts didn't go away, but thankfully the nausea was gone and I didn't have any severe panic attacks like I did that evening when Mom took me to the ER. For me, this confirmed that the medications were making the situation worse. But, now what do I do? How do I protect myself and my family?

I truly started to believe that I had become a psycho and felt like I was in a movie. "Is this what they feel like? Out of control with voices commanding and tempting them to do harmful things?" I thought to myself. As I continued to let my mind wander about people with mental health problems, I became sympathetic. I felt their pain, their suffering, and their hopelessness.

Then my mind wandered how they received help. "They are put in a psych ward", the voice interrupted. My heart sank at the thought. I felt like a failure and an embarrassment to my family. I didn't want my daughter to grow up with a crazy psycho mom.

But, somehow, the thought gave me some relief. If I was in a psych ward, I wouldn't be able to hurt anyone. I called my mom to see what her thoughts were. She mentioned that if I voluntarily turned myself in, then I could leave when I wanted. That thought made me feel better. It couldn't hurt to try and I was so desperate for answers and a way to make all of this go away.

So I looked up the closest mental health hospital and called them. But, the response I was given was unexpected.

Chapter 13

A sweet lady with a calming voice answered the phone. I explained to her that I felt like I needed to come receive help at their facility. I didn't hold back. I told her everything from the different visions I was seeing and the voice I was hearing. The intrusive thoughts of hurting myself and others, the constant fear, anxiety, panic attacks, lack of sleep, loss of appetite, brain fog, and that I felt unstable.

"I hear everything you are saying and I understand. Give me just a second. I am going to let you talk to Julia. Don't go anywhere", she said calmly. I thought that was strange. But, within a few seconds, I heard Julia answer. She also had a very calming and understanding tone. She asked me a few questions and then I spent another 15 minutes explaining everything a second time. “Have you ever attempted to hurt yourself or anyone else?” She asked. I took a second to think back on the last two and a half months. “No, ma'am,” I replied. She took another 10 minutes to ask me a few other questions.

“Courtney, I don’t think that you need to come in”, she calmly. “Oh”, is all that I said, and got quiet. I was confused. After all of the crazy and scary things I just told her, she doesn’t think I need to turn myself in to get help. “You haven’t done anything to hurt yourself or anyone else. It sounds like you are just scared of your thoughts”, she said. She explained her reasoning some more and reassured me that I was not psycho. But she thought it might be a good idea to see a doctor to get on anxiety medication to help me get through my day. “Oh no. I’ve already tried that”, I explained and told her about my awful experience. “I see. Have you tried counseling?” she asked. “No ma’am, I haven’t tried that yet”, I replied. “That may be a good place to start. But, please know that we are here if you have any more questions”, she said politely ending the conversation. I thanked her and ended the call.

That’s not at all how I thought that phone call was going to end. “I’m just scared of my thoughts?” Well, that might be more of a relief if I could only find a way to make the “thoughts” go away. I also assumed that she would understand since she was a professional. But, it felt more like she was trying to calm me down and make me feel better. Maybe other people don't hear what I am hearing. Maybe people don't have the visions that I've been having. Suddenly, I felt more alone than before. "I told you no one would believe you", the voice said interrupting my thoughts. My shoulders started to feel heavy and my heart felt defeated once again.

Over the next couple of weeks, I tried everything I could to avoid any harm that the voice prompted me to do. There were times when the voice tempted me to run off the road. So I had someone else drive me every chance I could. I had my family over as often as I could to help distract me from the thoughts and voice. I also realized that acts of service towards someone seemed to be a good distraction.

One night I gave my whole family a foot rub. Some of them tried reassuring me that I didn't need to rub their feet while other family members gladly accepted the offer. Either way, I didn't care. I was thankful for the distraction. I was also grateful for the copious amounts of grueling homework I had throughout each week that passed.

I was especially thankful for my friends, Livvy and Carly whom I commuted to school with every day. We got to know each other pretty quickly. Well, I got to know them. They didn't know about the things going on in my head. We had an hour commute each way and we had a lot of projects we completed together. The three of us became known as the Shermanettes during our two years at Texas Woman's University.

Looking on the outside, my life was exciting and I was rapidly achieving goals that I had worked relentlessly for. But, on the inside, I was exhausted by the constant torment of horrific visions and voices. My hope and optimism had officially run out.

Until one early morning, we were on the way to school. In the back seat of Livvy's Jeep, I had a vision that changed my life forever.

Chapter 14

For the first time, I didn't want to go to school. I was completely depleted of any energy or motivation to carry on. I wanted to give up. "There is a knife. You could end your life now and you would finally be able to rest", the voice said one early November morning. This time I took time to consider the thought. A strange relief and the heaviness in my shoulders lifted just a little as I considered being free from this mental prison. I wouldn't have to suffer anymore and I could finally relax. I've tried everything else I could think of.

I groaned at the thought and sluggishly got ready to leave the house by 5:15 am. One thing I hated was to let others down who depended on me or not show up to something I've committed myself to. Fortunately, those thoughts won over the voice and gave me what little motivation I could muster up to keep going.

It was still dark outside. Livvy was driving, Carly was in the passenger seat, and I was sitting in the tiny back seat of Livvy's two-door white Jeep Wrangler. I leaned my head against the window and looked out as far as I could see. I was mentally, emotionally, and physically worn out. I just wanted to close my eyes and take a nap until we got to school.

You would think after all these few months of seeing demonic visions, that I would get used to it or at least expect it. But, when I closed my eyes and laid my head against the window, this particular vision sent me off the edge. More dark figures came flying at me to attack what was left of me. I was outnumbered and I had no energy left to fight back. It felt like the air was being sucked out of me, my chest felt heavy, and it was hard to breathe. I quickly opened my eyes and in my head, I screamed "God I can't do this anymore!" My heart was racing, I felt faint and paralyzed all at the same time. I couldn't do anything but close my eyes. "No, not again," I thought as I braced myself for another evil vision.

But, for the first time in months, ever really, I did not see any demonic figures launching towards me. Instead, I saw a man walking towards me. He had hair down to his shoulders, he was wearing a robe with long sleeves, it was draped with different layers that came down to his feet, he wasn't wearing any shoes, and he was glowing bright yellow like the sun. I couldn't quite make out his facial features, but I was in complete awe of his beautiful glow. I didn't have to wonder who he was. Somehow, I immediately knew it was Jesus walking towards me even though I'd never seen Him before. There wasn't a sign telling me His name and He didn't have to tell me who He was. I just…knew.

The closer He got to me, the more peace, relief, and happiness I felt. Once He reached me, I realized I couldn't speak. I just stared at Him in desperation and hope. He gently reached down, placed one finger on my forehead and said, "Do not worry. You are saved and you are Mine". An overwhelming weight was physically lifted off my shoulders and my chest. At that moment, I was no longer scared. The authoritative, yet gentle tone He spoke in gave me confidence that He would take care of me. For the first time in my life, a wave of unexplainable peace came over me. Then, He was gone.

I opened my eyes and realized I was still curled up in the back seat of Livvy's Jeep. Both of the girls were sitting quietly in the front and neither of them were aware of what just happened. WOW!

I closed my eyes to see if I could still see Him, but He was gone and so were the dark evil figures. I longed for Him to come back, just so I could rest for a while in His presence. But, I left my eyes closed trying to focus on what I had just experienced and I cried in relief for the next 40 minutes on the way to school.

Throughout the rest of the day, the vision I had experienced in the back seat of Livvy's Jeep preoccupied my thoughts. It felt more real life-like than a "vision". I could see Him, I heard Him speak, and I felt the light gentle pressure as He put his finger on my forehead. I clung to the peace and rest that I felt during the short experience. The hope that He gave me somehow overpowered and demolished all the panic attacks, the fear, and the constant state of anxiety. I didn't want it to go away.

Chapter 15

For the next several days, I would intentionally think about hurting someone. Why? I wanted to see if it would cause any panic or fear. Or, if it was all finally over. I realized, after my face-to-face moment with Jesus, that I no longer had constant fear or random temptations that I would hurt someone. I could finally breathe.

Unfortunately, random thoughts about me committing suicide still occurred. I don't recall hearing a voice anymore, which was a relief. However, I was confused as to why I still had suicidal thoughts and I wasn't sure how to make the thoughts go away.

One day after school, I broke down and explained a few things to Carly and Livvy. We were in Carly's white sedan. Carly was driving, I was in the passenger seat, and Livvy was sitting in the middle of the backseat listening intentionally. I gave them enough information to give them an idea of the anxiety I had been having, but I did not dare tell them the voice I heard or the constant demonic things that I had seen. I also never told them about my encounter with Jesus. I wasn't sure if they would think that I was crazy or believe me.

I was just hoping to confide in my friends and hope they might have some advice. After opening up to Livvy and Carly, I quickly realized there was a reason for going to TWU and a reason. God had placed us all three together. God knew I would need friends during this time who could sympathize, knew how to listen, and never once had a judgemental tone towards me. They only offered the mental and emotional support that I needed to help me get through school.

Carly also mentioned that she heard good things about a doctor on the TWU campus who helped students experiencing anxiety. I instantly felt my chest tighten at the thought of seeing another doctor. Especially, after what happened the last time I took medication for anxiety. I gave my friends a brief overview of my concerns about being on any medication and that I was determined to be able to combat and control this without any medications.

I was so grateful that Livvy and Carly were both very understanding. Carly explained that I could think about it and if I changed my mind, she would go with me for support. She said I could explain my last experience to the doctor and ask if I could start by taking the lowest dose to see if I had any undesirable side effects. While I didn't want to be on medication, her last statement gave me some hope. Besides, even if I decided to go see this doctor, it didn't mean I had to take medication. Maybe he had other options.

I had a few days to think about it before making an appointment. I found out that this doctor had a good reputation for helping students get through school who suffered from anxiety and depression. I discussed it with my family and they were supportive of whichever decision I made. So, I cautiously decided to give this new doctor a try. As Carly promised, she drove with me an hour away to see if this doctor could find a way to help reduce my anxiety. I was so grateful for her friendship and understanding.

At the doctor's office, I sat in the small room waiting as my heart raced. I couldn't stop thinking about my last experience taking medication that had me sitting in the ER parking lot. And worse, the medical professionals didn't believe me. What if this time it isn't any different?

There was a knock on the door and I was greeted by an older gentleman gently smiling at me. "Hello, Courtney. The ladies told me you were having some anxiety", he said. His calm demeanor slowed my heart rate and I was able to relax. "Yes, sir", I replied. I gave him a brief overview of the last three months. I did not give him as many details as I did the previous doctor who was smirking behind his hand. I didn't want this doctor to think I was crazy, but I did want him to know the severity of my anxiety and depression. I also expressed my concern with taking medication long-term and my horrific experience the last time a doctor prescribed me medication.

He gently nodded his head in understanding while he jotted some notes down on his paperwork. "Let's try Celexa. I know you are concerned with the side effects, so I will prescribe the lowest dose there is. For the first couple of days, break the pill in half. If you feel like your anxiety or depression is getting worse, I want you to call me. I have many students who do well on this medication, so I am hoping you will too", he said in his gentle tone. "Also, it is very important that you get in to see a counselor. You shouldn't be going through this alone", he stated in a firm, caring tone.

I thanked him and promised I would call if things got worse. As we left the doctor's office, I felt so much relief. He gave me confidence that he believed the anxiety and depression I was having. He was also gentle and understanding without making me feel like I was crazy.

That evening, I made sure my family knew I was trying a new medication and to watch out for any heightened emotions coming from me. I was nervous as I broke the tiny 10mg pill in half. I was having more flashbacks from the last time I took anxiety medication. But, I was hopeful as I drank some water making sure the pill went down. I spent some time with my daughter, ate dinner, and went to bed.

The next morning, I woke up expecting to feel nauseous, brain fog, or some increase in fear. Surprisingly, none of those things occurred. Thank the Lord! I still felt some anxiety, but the medication didn't make it worse. So, I continued with the instructions the doctor gave me and took the other half of the pill I had broken the night before.

For the next few days, I noticed that I was a little more clear-headed. Unfortunately, the suicidal thoughts didn't go away. But, when they randomly popped up in my head, I realized I didn't have a panic attack. I also, noticed that I still hadn't heard the voice since my encounter with Jesus. Was the voice finally gone?! I wasn't sure, but I made a mental note and decided to focus on the small positive improvements. Once I was confident that the medication was not causing any negative side effects, I started taking the full 10mg dose.

There was one instance since I started taking Celexa when I had an intense anxiety attack. After a couple of months of taking it, we were out of town at a conference for the weekend. All of the girls seemed so excited to get away for the weekend as we took our luggage up to our hotel rooms. In this particular hotel, the center of it was open like you would see at a mall. I could see down to the lobby and the room doors across the other side. The elevators were glass and we could see the people inside riding to the top floor. The hotel was very beautiful and impressive.

Apart from the random suicidal thoughts, I was excited to be there. Until we got to the fourth floor of the hotel. As we got off the elevator, I could see the beautiful fountain and indoor trees at the very bottom, and I had a random thought to throw myself over the railing that came up to my waist. I froze internally at the thought. My heart started to race and chills ran up and down my spine as I started to feel queasy. “No!” I screamed internally as I moved away from the railing as far as possible.

I couldn’t get to the hotel room fast enough. I don’t think any of my classmates noticed my panic attack as they were all still in awe of the beautiful hotel. Once we reached the hotel room, I took a few minutes to calm down and reason that I never would do such a thing.

I looked in the bathroom mirror and had mixed emotions. I lost a lot of weight, which was nice. But, it was too much weight. You could see my clavicle and the top three ribs in my chest. My face almost looked hollow and I had dark circles under my eyes. I don’t think I had ever looked this thin before. I changed into comfortable clothes that hid my skeletal figure and touched up my makeup to bring some life back into my face.

Once I was calm and after some small talk with my friends, we decided to go downstairs. At first, I was afraid the thought would come back if I left the room and could see the railing. But, I was so tired of being intimidated by random things. So, as we left the room and started walking, I stayed away from the railing and practically walked up against the wall.

At some point, someone motioned for me to come over to the railing to look at something pretty. I slowly walked over to the railing. I wasn't able to pay attention to what they were pointing to as the thought of throwing myself over the railing came back. Instead of panicking or running away, I held on to the railing and stared at the bottom floor until the thought went away.

"Are you coming, Corndog?", Carly said. I was given the nickname Corndog on the first day of school due to my name being misspelled in the TWU school system. Her voice broke my concentration, but since my anxiety eased up, I decided to go downstairs with my friends. Besides, it was nice to get away from the railing. Thankfully, each time I walked around the fourth floor, the thought of going over the railing faded more each time and it was a nice distraction spending time with my friends with all the meetings and activities throughout the weekend.

After that incident, I never had an intense urge to commit suicide. Random thoughts would occur, but I was able to carry forward without letting the thought ruin my day. It was obvious that Celexa was helping me get through each day as my anxiety did not linger when a thought popped into my head.

For the next six months my classes, homework, community service, my family and friends also helped to preoccupy my mind and kept me motivated to move forward. I was beyond grateful for each one of them as they were more helpful to me than they will ever know.

Chapter 16

Six months had passed by this point and I was determined to wean myself off of the Celexa. My doctor instructed me to never stop taking the medication cold turkey, so I decided to break the pills in half until I ran out.

I continued going to school and stayed close to my friends and family. They never knew how thankful I was to have them in such a desperate time in my life. I was also grateful that I did not have any side effects and my anxiety never got worse once I stopped taking Celexa. Finally! I was able to achieve my goal of controlling my anxiety and thoughts without needing any medication. It was a big accomplishment for me and it gave me a little more confidence in myself.

Unfortunately, I still had random thoughts of suicide throughout the next six months. I realized that some things would trigger thoughts such as stressing about school or being by myself for too long in certain environments. Thankfully, I was able to get through the thoughts without hurting myself or having a panic attack. I also did my best to prevent any triggers by surrounding myself with positive people and finding different ways to laugh throughout the day.

Unfortunately, there was a certain time frame during my last semester at TWU that I decided to seek professional help to get through some thoughts and emotions.

Right before I started my last semester my husband expressed his desire to make a significant lifestyle change. He was nervous to tell me, afraid that I may not want anything to do with the change. I wanted him to be happy, but he was right. I didn't want anything to do with the path he decided to take.

It wasn't what I wanted for my life and honestly, nothing about it felt "natural" or normal. Even though I knew our marriage was coming to an end, it wasn't an easy decision. There were so many variables to consider. We had been married for nine years, we had a daughter together who was only four years old at the time, and I needed to finish school.

I was trying to wrap my head around what was happening. This was the last thing I needed. Everything at home was secretly falling apart while my school workload increased, I prepared for my board exam, along with multiple community events, and meetings.

It was way too much to process at once. I didn't give him a true answer for several weeks. But, I finally told Tyler that there was no future for us with his new lifestyle choice and we needed to get divorced. He didn't argue with me, but it was very evident that my decision to leave was crushing him. I had agreed to be the one to move out, but it was complicated since I was still in school with no income. Plus, we had Elaina to think about.

We both agreed I would continue living in the house until I graduated and was able to save enough money to move out. We respected each other's personal space while I stayed in the master bedroom and he slept in his game room. While we were now only roommates, we tried our best to keep everything else as normal as possible for Elaina's sake.

But, it didn't make anything easier. I became overwhelmed with so many emotions that I stopped carpooling with Livvy and Carly, and I didn't spend any extra time with them unless it was necessary. Mostly, because I cried so much and I didn't know how to explain the strange and sudden chaos going on outside of school. My heart was heavy with devastation. The weight of everything going on was causing unwanted thoughts and severe anxiety to creep back in. How was I going to be able to stay focused and disciplined to get through school?

One of my good friends recommended a counselor for me to confide in to help me through the process. It dawned on me that I never took my doctor's advice in the beginning to seek someone for professional help. But, I didn’t feel like I needed medication for this situation.

Even though all of this was a lot and it made me sad, it was still nothing compared to me seeing demonic visions and hearing voices. I wouldn’t wish that traumatic three months on my worst enemy. All of this seemed like a piece of cake compared to that and I felt like I could handle it without taking medication. So, I settled for my friend's advice and called the counselor with what little time commitment I could find.

I explained everything to the counselor the first time I met her. She was kind and gentle but was understanding as she had also gone through a divorce. By the end of our first session, we were able to identify my biggest concern that was causing anxiety. Elaina. What would happen to her? How do we explain all of this to a four-year-old and how will our decisions affect her long-term?

The thought of Elaina being negatively affected made me cry every time I thought about it. Which was frequent.

I would cry during my hour drive to and from school. And it consumed my thoughts so much that Livvy pointed it out one day at school.

"Courtney, is everything okay? You seem sad or distracted", Livvy said. We were in a quiet computer lab trying to complete homework assignments that continued to pile up on us. She was sitting across the table from me and we were currently the only ones left in the room. I didn't want to tell her what was going on. I looked up to acknowledge her but stayed silent. She closed her laptop and shoved it aside. All attention was on me and it was obvious she wasn't giving in. She stayed quiet while I looked down. Tears slowly started to form in my eyes as I quietly uttered, “I can’t even get myself to say it out loud”.

It has been about two weeks since I’ve spent any alone time with Livvy. We had become very close. Best friends even. But, I had mixed emotions that I didn’t know how to deal with. I felt… embarrassed, ashamed, taken advantage of, sad, lonely, confused, deceived, overwhelmed with concern for Elaina, and overstimulated with the ridiculous amounts of homework.

I looked up. She was looking at me concerned, still waiting for me to spill the beans. I took another long pause and finally came out with it. “Tyler told me a couple of weeks ago that… he… has decided to become a woman”, I said in an embarrassed whisper.

I didn’t hear a response, so I looked up to see her eyes wide. “Courtney, I’m really sorry… is there anything I can do?” Wiping my eyes I replied, “No, but thank you. I know I have been distant, but it’s because I don’t know what to say and every time I think about it I start to cry. Please don’t tell anyone. I don’t want anyone asking questions and I don't want to think about it. I just need to focus on getting through this last semester. It’s the only thing I know to do right now. It is also the reason I have decided to drive separately to and from school lately.”

She smiled and opened her laptop back up. “You have my word. But, you will let me know if you need anything or someone to talk to, right?” she said. I smiled back at her and nodded my head “Yes”. Wow, somehow I felt so much relief just by confiding in my best friend. I was also able to focus a little better in class. However, I still cried during my commute to and from school when I was alone with my thoughts.

After a couple of more sessions with my counselor, she asked if there was any improvement. I admitted that I cried a lot and explained the worst times were when I was driving alone. At the end of the session, she walked me to the door, hugged me, and bluntly said, "You need fresh air. Take daily walks even if it is only five minutes a day. Oh, and NO MORE CRYING". I looked at her confused. She smiled at me, gave me another hug, and said, "Seriously, no more crying. Okay?" I nodded my head yes and got in my car. I sat there quietly for a few minutes, contemplating what she said.

Chapter 17

It seemed strange that a counselor would tell someone "No more crying". However, the blunt instructions felt motivating to me. It's like I needed it. I needed someone to help snap me out of the self-pity that I had dug myself into. It was evident the constant crying was doing nothing for me except making the situation worse, stealing my joy, and preventing me from being emotionally productive.

So, I took my counselor's advice quite literally. I made a point to find time to take a walk outside. I was a little nervous at first walking alone down a country road by myself. But, after 10 minutes of getting my heart rate up and looking far out over some pretty rolling hills, I noticed I felt more relaxed and less stressed. This gave me the motivation to find time the next day to go for another walk. I even made a point to take the stairs instead of the elevator at school or to use my lunchtime to take a walk.

Also, I refused to cry when I was alone by looking at my current situation from a different perspective. Was life at home wacky? YES. But, I'm not hearing voices! I'm not seeing demonic visions! I only have a few months of school left and I will be free from loads of homework! I have my sweet, sweet Elaina and I have the best support system! The most exciting thing that I couldn't dismiss was the fact I got to be face-to-face with Jesus! It was the most miraculous thing that has ever happened to me and I still cling to it to this very day (seven years later).

That experience had changed my life. The overwhelming peace I felt during those 30 seconds could never dull a bad situation when I think about Jesus. What He looked like, what He said to me, the fear He broke off me, and the indescribable peace and love I felt… nothing can compare! I found myself thinking about Him more and more when I was alone and I started to look forward to my daily walks with Him.

Then it dawned on me. **Jesus has been the missing piece this whole time!**

After two weeks of spending my alone time thinking about Him, I realized I hadn't cried, had an anxiety attack, a panic attack, or felt overly stressed.

I spent so much time trying to "fix" or "prevent" my stress and anxiety. Yet, the "fix" and the "prevention" was Jesus this whole time. It didn't matter what I tried: medication, counseling, confiding in family, seeking doctors and mental institutions, a margarita, comedy, school, and any other distraction I could think of. Some of those things might have eased the torment or anxiety, but it didn't make it go completely away. The only thing that made those things go away, was when I kept my thoughts on Jesus and the peace and love He exudes. I felt…FREE. Life at home and school became "easy" to handle.

Jesus. The thought of Him got me thinking about what my next step would be during this uncertain season.

I didn't know what my future here on earth would hold, but what I did know was that I had an eternity in Heaven and I even had a glimpse of what it would feel like. I knew I was saved, but it dawned on me…I still hadn't been baptized.

Chapter 18

Despite the demands of my last semester of school, I made it my mission to find a church where I could feel that same presence of His love and peace. But, I didn't know how or where to start. I didn't grow up in church, but I did take advantage if a friend or family member invited me.

I didn't know anything about the Bible or scripture. I had felt the urge to start reading the Bible many times throughout my childhood and young adult years, but never made it past Genesis 2. Once I got past how God created the heavens and the earth, my eyes would glaze over and I couldn't comprehend what I was reading. So, unfortunately, I would give up.

With that said, growing up if anyone mentioned Jesus or God, they had my full attention and I wanted to know everything they had to say about Him. Unfortunately, most of the time I couldn't comprehend what they were talking about.

But now, I didn't need other people to tell me what He was like. I only had 30 seconds with Him and I knew.

So I church-hopped for a month or two. I have been to all kinds of churches. I had mostly visited Baptist churches in the past, but I've also been to Cowboy, Mormon, Pentecostal, Catholic, undenominational, and one or two other churches. I was running out of recommendations for what church I should visit, but I wasn't giving up! I knew there was a church where I was supposed to be. I could feel it. In hindsight, I know it was the Lord keeping church doors closed until He got me where He wanted me. How do I know?

One day I asked my mom where a church was located that we had visited years before. Lo and behold it was only about 20 miles from where I lived at the time. So, the next Sunday, one of my good friends, Andrea, and I went to visit King's Trail Cowboy Church. I was a little intimidated at first because there were so many people and neither of us knew anyone attending there.

After 30 minutes of worship, Pastor Jason Norton got behind the pulpit, prayed and within ten minutes of his preaching I knew that's exactly where I was supposed to be. Not only did I feel that same Holy Spirit peace that I felt when I met Jesus, but he was also talking about things that I had experienced. Things I couldn't explain when I was going through the demonic attack! I had never met Jason Norton, yet he talked as if he had been through something very similar and I knew that if I were to say something to him, he would one hundred percent believe me. He also discussed how to protect and fight demonic or spiritual attacks, which left me feeling so much more hope. I had never heard someone preaching like he did! I never heard anyone talk about things unseen, spirits, or anxiety like he did. He also spoke in a manner that was easy for me to understand by explaining or giving examples that correlated with scripture.

I couldn't wait to go back next Sunday. I knew that was where I wanted and NEEDED to get baptized. So, Andrea and I got up the next Sunday and went. But, this time, it was Pastor Duane Wegley preaching, and toward the end of his sermon, he mentioned baptism. As he prayed everyone out, I started praying, "Jesus for the first time ever, I know I am supposed to get baptized and I know it's supposed to be here. Please give me the courage and confidence to talk to the right person so I can schedule my baptism". At that time, Pastor Duane said something about baptism and a lady named Tina who sits in the back. Wow, that was quick. Thank You, Jesus and Duane!

I was so nervous to walk through the huge crowd of people to find a lady I never met. But, I knew, that I knew, that I knew what I was supposed to do and I didn't want to put it off any longer.

I looked at Andrea and said, "I have to go find a lady named Tina". She nodded and followed me. We weaved in and out of the sea of people trying to make our way to this Tina lady who was supposed to be in the back of the sanctuary. When we got to the back, a pretty lady with glasses and a short spikey hairstyle greeted us with a smile.

"Hey girls, how are y'all doing?" she said with a sweet southern accent. "Yes, could you please tell me where I can find Tina?" I replied. "Oh, you just missed her, she is talking with some other folks at the moment. My name is Candy, is there something I can help with?" she asked. "I would like to sign up and schedule my baptism please," I said eagerly. She stood up, took her glasses off, and said "You know for sure that you want to get baptized?" I smiled big, "Yes, ma'am I do". She walked around the desk, grabbed my hand, and said "Follow me."

I looked back at Andrea with a confused smile as Candy led me back towards the stage. "Oh, my bad. Did I go to the wrong desk? I thought Pastor Duane said to meet with Tina in the back?" I said with a confused smile. "If you know you want to get baptized, then we won't leave until you are," she said with excitement, still holding my hand and weaving around the crowd. Still confused, I asked, "Wait, so I don't have to make an appointment, have counseling with the pastor, and schedule a day for friends and family to come to witness my baptism?" "Oh, no honey. We don't wait to get baptized. If you know you want to, then you do it right then", she said as we approached the stairs to the baptismal.

I filled out my baptismal form and was instructed to take off my shoes. I could feel my cheeks start to turn pink with embarrassment as I could feel people looking at me. I hated being the center of attention and I also started to question if today was the right day. I didn't feel as if I was dressed appropriately to be baptized. I had this whole thing “planned” out in my head. You know, wear a loose dark shirt, dark pants or shorts, bring a change of clothes, a towel, and wear waterproof makeup.

That morning I had spent quite a bit of time doing my makeup and hair, wearing jeans, a fitted black turtleneck with an army green jacket, and black ankle boots. While I was grateful that Andrea was with me to witness my baptism, I didn’t have any of my family with me. That thought created more doubt as I was instructed to walk up the stairs followed by a sweet lady carrying a towel for me.

As I walked up the stairs, I started to feel slightly nervous, followed by an overwhelming peace. I no longer cared what other people thought, what I was wearing, that

I didn't have any clothes to change into, or that my family wasn't there. Not because I don't love them, but because I realized this was for me. Not anyone else. I knew Jesus was real because I saw Him, I felt His presence full of peace and joy that I never wanted to end. I wanted to be as close to Him as possible and if this was how it needed to happen, then so be it. I couldn't wait to feel His presence again!

Pastor Duane and an elder helped me into the baptismal. Remember, this is a Cowboy church, so this was not a bathtub or a fancy pool with a glass wall for the witnesses to see. This baptismal was a huge galvanized horse water trough full of water and we are in the country so there are random pieces of grass floating around and pieces of…dirt I think. And the water was slightly cool for me. (I am one of those people who like their water almost scorching.) Wow, this was not what I had pictured for my “perfect” baptism. But, all I could think about was seeing Jesus again and feeling His peaceful presence I felt a year and a half ago.

Pastor Duane asked a few questions and then asked if I believed and confessed that Jesus is Lord and God raised Him from the dead. I smiled, nodded my head, and said, “Yes, for the first time, I know He is”. He gave a slight smile and he and the other elder gently lowered me down below the water and pulled me back up.

I don’t know what I was expecting when I came up out of the water. I had imagined that I would rush up out of the water screaming and crying full of joy! But, it was the opposite. I was quiet as the gentleman helped me out of the horse trough and I had a wave of unbelief that maybe it didn't work. It was nothing like I had seen when others were baptized and I didn't have a face-to-face with Jesus that I thought I would see.

I felt a towel being wrapped around me and someone helped me walk down the stairs. I looked down and I saw Andrea's beautiful face smiling and beaming with joy as she clapped for me. I awkwardly walked toward her with my clothes dripping water everywhere and put on my boots. She hugged me and we said our goodbyes as we walked outside to our separate vehicles.

I got in my car and sat there quietly while my clothes got my seat soaking wet, but I didn't care. I was more concerned that I couldn't feel the presence of Jesus. So, I prayed and asked Him why I didn't feel His joy and if I did it too soon. It didn't make sense. I KNEW that was the next thing I needed to do, but I wasn't an expert at knowing how to do it. I barely knew anything about baptism or Jesus except that He was real and He would protect me because I belonged to Him.

After a while of contemplating my choice to get baptized today, I started my car and decided to leave. As I was exiting the parking lot, everything that just happened and in the specific sequence came rushing into my mind and I was immediately flooded with the joy and peace that I was craving from Jesus.

He revealed to me that He was gently and patiently guiding me to that specific church on that specific day. He specifically gave me the confidence to seek who could baptize me which He revealed as soon as I prayed for it at the end of the sermon. He knew my desire to be as close as I could to Him. He revealed each step that happened within the last 30 minutes was specifically orchestrated by Him. He also revealed He knows everything I'm thinking and my desires. But He explained to me that there is nothing "routine" about being close to Him or "routine" about getting baptized. He flooded my heart with so much love, peace, and joy that I broke down crying alone in my car. He also revealed to me that being saved and baptized is an intimate connection between Him and me. It is not something that is required to have an audience who witnesses or cheers me on. It is also not something that I "planned" and scheduled myself. That is considered passive thinking rather than faithful thinking.

He was gently teaching me He knows all things and that His ways are higher than mine. But, Jesus never once condemned or made me feel guilty. Instead, He covered me with comforting joy and encouraged me to rely on His timing and guidance.

Jesus is the BEST teacher.

Chapter 19

I want to leave you with these closing thoughts. If you struggle with anxiety, depression, loneliness, addiction, or demonic or spiritual attacks that you can't explain, please know you're not alone.

If you have tried explaining your situation to someone but they don't understand or know how to help and probably think you're crazy, you must know I believe you! We can't expect others to know what we see or feel if they have never had these experiences. Here is where you show grace and mercy to others.

If you are not advanced in the Word of God, then you may be like me when I was experiencing these things. I was not aware that the enemy would make me feel secluded, crazy, and like no one would believe me. I was not aware that this was what a demonic attack felt like. I didn't even know things like this existed or that the enemy would do whatever he could to take you out.

I did not know that the enemy comes to kill, steal, and destroy whatever he can (John 10:10). I learned that God did not give "us a spirit of fear, but of power and of love and of a sound mind" (2 Timothy 1:7). So if fear or anxiety starts to creep in, you can immediately identify that it is not of God and it is not His will for you to feel that way. How do you get it to go away? Turn your attention back to Jesus when you start to feel anxious. You can do this by turning on worship music, directly talking to Him and saying how you feel, or reading His words in the Bible. James 4:7 states if you submit to God, it is an act of resisting the devil. If you do this, he will flee from you and you will start to feel peace. Do not be discouraged if it takes more than a few minutes. Keep going and resisting! Even Jesus had to resist the devil.

I didn't know that the devil was trying to take me out before I knew that I was chosen by God and that I have an inheritance (Ephesians 1:4 and 1:11).

I pray for encouragement for whoever is reading this. Know that if you feel like you're hitting rock bottom and your situation seems hopeless, then the devil has you right where he wants you. Where is the encouragement, you ask? It is simple.

The devil is trying to take you out because he knows you are important, you are chosen, and if you have the Holy Spirit inside of you, then you have power over the devil. (Luke 10:19). He doesn't want me, you or anyone else to know that information.

I want to take you back to Chapter 9 when I was convinced there was a rifle in the hallway. The enemy is a liar and a deceiver. He knew I had a fear of using a gun to hurt myself or someone else. The enemy used it to keep me bound in fear and anxiety. The only reason the enemy knew I was scared of the false vision of a gun, is because I allowed him to. You see, the enemy can not hear your thoughts. Only God can.

How does the enemy know if you are afraid or worried about something? The enemy will whisper something in your ear and will wait to see how you respond. Did you panic or become anxious at the thought? Did you start talking out loud about how scared you are? If yes, then the enemy will use it to his advantage any chance he can.

My point in saying this is to encourage you to stand firm regardless if you are scared of something. If I had not responded in fear, by saying it out loud and leaping past the gun cabinet, then the enemy never would have known.

If you have Jesus as your Lord and Savior and the Holy Spirit lives inside you, then you have the power to rebuke any unwanted thoughts, in Jesus' name! There is life and death in words you speak (Proverbs 18: 21).

I learned from Terri Savelle Foy, a quick way to examine if I am speaking death over myself. After every sentence say "And that's just the way I want it". When I started saying that phrase after every sentence, I quickly learned how to speak positive declarations over my life and it began to change my perspective! For example, I might say "I am never going to lose weight and that's just the way I want it". It brings awareness that it's not my true goal and therefore shouldn't be speaking in that manner. Instead, I should say, "I'm going to lose 20 pounds by April 7th and that's just the way I want it!" That simple change is much more inspiring and motivating.

Please also remember, that I didn't have any energy or any fight left in me. I was ready to give up because I felt so weak and exhausted. It only took enough energy to cry out to God, and Jesus showed up. Not any other "god" or religious idol to save me. It was Jesus.

I also had an immediate breakthrough and knew everything was going to be okay. It took time for me to have complete healing and confidence. I had to keep seeking Jesus, keep talking to Him, keep reading His words and teachings, and seek like-minded believers who encouraged me to stay on the right path. The more I learned about Jesus the closer I got to Him. This made it easier for me to know when He was speaking to me and guiding me (John 10:14)!

I want to point out I had two different opportunities to be prayed over when I was being demonically tormented. Unfortunately, the enemy whispered fear in my ears and I turned down the prayers. I don't like to dwell on this, but I share it in case anyone may be going through something unexplainable and scary. It made me think, would I have encountered Jesus sooner if I had accepted the prayers?

Even though this was the hardest and scariest time of my life, I am glad it happened to me and I don't resent any part of it. Some of you might be scratching your head asking yourselves, Why would she be happy about something so horrific?

Because, it brought me to the most peaceful 30 seconds of my life that I will always cherish. It put me face-to-face with Jesus. All of my questions like, is Jesus real? What does Jesus look like? Am I truly saved and going to Heaven? All answered in a matter of seconds when I was convinced it was over and would end up taking my life.

Moving forward we must ask the Lord for discernment when we are going about our daily lives. Remember in Chapter 2 when I recommended not watching the “It” movie? That goes for anything that we are entertaining. Such as music, movies, TV series, concerts, people we hang around, and places that we go.

For example, I love funny movies and stand-up comedy. However, when I started following Jesus, He revealed to me that certain movies and shows I watched were planting "bad seeds" that could later manifest and be used by the enemy to trap me in anxiety and depression.

I may get opposing opinions about this, but I used to love the show Grey's Anatomy. One night about three years ago, I was watching it and I got the overwhelming feeling to turn it off and stop watching the show altogether. The drama, the immoral sex scenes, the sad scenes, etc. immediately made me feel…icky and gross.

Once I stopped watching it, the Lord revealed that I must always protect myself from what I am watching, hearing, and the places I am going (Proverbs 4:20-27). At first, I was worried that I wouldn't be able to have any entertainment or fun but I started to realize within a month or so the exact opposite happened. I noticed I didn't get as many mood swings and I didn't get easily sad or depressed. I felt more peaceful and happy once I started to eliminate things that included foul language, drama, sexual immorality, drugs, drinking, innuendos, and subliminal messages.

Don't give in to the schemes and lies of the enemy. Be encouraged! There is a breakthrough right on the other side of what you're going through. The good news is you don't have to do it alone.

You have a choice. If you want to ask Jesus to be Lord over your life, He promises to send an "advocate to help you and be with you forever" (John 14:16). The Holy Spirit who lives in you, intercedes and fights for you continuously.

Cry out to God and He will sustain you, help you thrive and prosper in doing amazing things that He has created you to do. Following Jesus is anything but boring! Remember, He will give you the desires of your heart in a manner that you never would have dreamed!

A Guide to Thrive

1. Ask Jesus to be your Lord and Savior (Romans 10:9-14) You DO NOT need someone to speak this over you and it doesn’t have to be in a church. Remember, I was in the back seat of my best friend's Jeep when I was saved. It is between you and Jesus. He will meet you right where you are!

2. Protect yourself from the lies and tricks of the enemy by putting on the full armor of God and being in prayer against the enemy’s schemes (Ephesians 6:11-18).

3. Renew your mind and wash yourself spiritually by reading God's word every day. It's like eating food to nourish your spirit!

4. Do not let the enemy win by letting unwanted thoughts control you. Remember, YOU are in control of your thoughts (if you have Jesus). It is important to know, apart from Him we can do nothing (John 15:5-8). If there is something that pops up in your mind that causes fear or depression, simply say, I rebuke those things in Jesus' name. Devil get away from me and go back to the pits of hell where you belong and don't come back!" Watch how fast it works!

5. Ask Him for discernment throughout each day when watching TV, listening to music, places you go, etc. Take note if death or life is being spoken in the things you are entertaining or do you get an uneasy feeling? These could be signs that He is trying to warn and protect you from being deceived by the enemy. Be careful NOT to quench the Holy Spirit (1 Thessalonians 5:19). He is there to help keep you on the right path, to prosper, and to do great things that you are called to do!
6. Make time to listen to worship music and watch an encouraging sermon or podcast you enjoy every day. More importantly, stay in

communication with Jesus every day by telling Him your concerns and desires. Then take a few minutes to be quiet and wait for Jesus to respond. Act in faith by having a pen and paper to write down what Jesus says!

7. Put your phone away and get fresh air! I cannot stress this enough. Make a point to open a window, sit outside, or go for a peaceful drive. It would be even better if you could go for a 10-30 minute walk. Physical movement allows you to release stress and increase happiness!

8. My friend, you were not created for darkness. You were created for a greater purpose and He is calling "You out of the darkness into His

marvelous light" (1 Peter 2:9). It's time to thrive and have fun doing it!

Made in the USA
Columbia, SC
28 April 2025

57259506R00093